Imprint:

Copyright © 2016 GRIN Verlag
Print and binding: Books on Demand GmbH, Norderstedt Germany
ISBN: 9783668638846

This book at GRIN:

https://www.grin.com/document/385753

Patrick Haug

Cloud Computing one of the success factors for Industry 4.0

Strategic and economic aspects

GRIN Verlag

GRIN - Your knowledge has value

Since its foundation in 1998, GRIN has specialized in publishing academic texts by students, college teachers and other academics as e-book and printed book. The website www.grin.com is an ideal platform for presenting term papers, final papers, scientific essays, dissertations and specialist books.

Visit us on the internet:

http://www.grin.com/

http://www.facebook.com/grincom

http://www.twitter.com/grin_com

***** University of Applied Science Essen

Location *****

Occupational Integration Study Path:
International Management (B.A.)

6th Semester
Term Paper in Strategic Management (S)

Cloud Computing one of the success factors for Industry 4.0.
Strategic and economic aspects.

Name: Patrick Haug
Delivery: 2016/08/10

Table of Contents

List of Figures

List of Tables

Abbreviations

CPS = Cyper physical systems

DaaS = Data-Storage as a service

ES = Embedded systems

GDP = Gross domestic product

IoT = Internet of things

IT = Information technology

NPV = Net present value

PaaS = Platform as a service

RoI = Return of investment

SaaS = Software as a service

TCO = Total cost of ownership

VaS = Value at stake

1 Introduction

Powered by hydro- and steam-power, at the end of the 18th century mechanical production facilities began to replace human labour. What is today known as the Industrial Revolution allowed for a more efficient use of resources such as labour and soil. At the same time, it was the corner stone for the increased use of capital as a resource. Figure 1 shows the impact of industrialization on gross domestic product (GDP).[1]

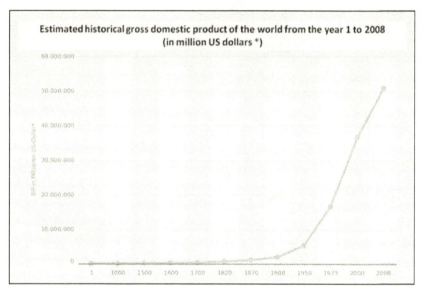

Figure 1: Historical gross domestic product of the world

Source: www.statista.com (A) (2016)

During the second Industrial Revolution towards the end of the 19th century manual labour was replaced by mass production (as developed by Frederick Winslow Taylor) and the introduction of assembly-line work (promoted by Henry Ford). The introduction of electronic control systems and information technology in the 1970s finally heralded the third Industrial Revolution.[2]

All three Industrial Revolutions until today have brought about accelerated processes and a degree of automation. In an increasingly global market, the Internet of Things (products, production facilities, tools) connects the real and the virtual world and Cyber Physical Systems (CPS) are the foundation of the fourth Industrial Revolution (Industry 4.0 – see Figure 2). CPS is an umbrella term for software-intensive embedded systems (ES) which are

---

[1] Cf. Dorst, W. (2012). p. 34.
[2] Cf. Härting, R. et. al. (2005). p. 9.

1

based on connected, integrated hardware- and software components in products or industrial production facilities (smart production) that are able to communicate with each other.[3]

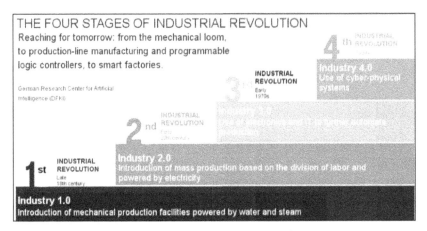

Figure 2: The four stages of the Industrial Revolution

Source: www.bestemnetwork.com (2016).

Cloud Computing in this context is the enabler with regards to the architectural requirements of smart factories which in turn are the basis of Industry 4.0.[4]

The aim of this term paper is to outline the opportunities and risks connected with the introduction of cloud systems. In addition to the strategic aspect the term paper will evaluate the economic aspect of cloud strategies by examining how to adapt the Total Cost of Ownership (TCO) method to suit cloud services.

The first chapters of this paper will present the underlying relationships between Industry 4.0, Internet of Things (IoT), Smart Production and the underlying technology stack behind, followed by an overview of the cloud solutions available as of today. This paper then evaluates the strategic potential of cloud strategies before finally providing a valuation model to deal with the challenge of ascertaining the economic potential of cloud solutions.

The first objective of the term paper work is to evaluate the potential of a cloud strategy based on SWOT analysis. The second key question is how to adapt and extend information technology typical commercial valuation models to a cloud strategy based business case.

---

[3] Cf. Dorst, W. (2012). p. 34.
[4] Cf. Porter, E. & Heppelmann, J. (2015). p. 100.

2 Drivers of Industry 4.0

2.1 Internet of Things

Thanks to wireless communication technology and the internet, nowadays, technical products, components, sensors, software and machines can be connected with each other. Via these connections they are able to exchange information and interact. For business and the industry sector the most apparent consequences will occur in fields like:

- automation,
- industrial manufacturing,
- logistics,
- business/process management,
- intelligent transportation of people and goods.[5]

Particularly the capabilities of collecting data and communicating it, are the basis for a number of far-reaching, innovative concepts which allow manufacturers to obtain much more detailed feedback on the use of their products. Based on this information, the design of products can be improved and short- as well as long-term conclusions, with regards to the production process, can be drawn. Such solutions, apart from connectivity requirements, also require the underlying systems to possess Big Data functionality.[6]

2.2 Aspects of Industry 4.0

It exist different possibilities to create value through the industrial use of IoT. The referenced architecture model of VDI/VDE society presents four main approaches (see figure 3).[7]

Horizontal Integration along value chain[8]

Horizontal integration is based on vertical integration. It allows for technical processes to be integrated into overarching business process and to be synchronized in real-time with other participants.

Vertical integration, e.g. within a factory/production site[9]

Vertical integration is the first stage and contains the entire cross-linked communication within a company. It ensures that the IT systems of different hierarchical levels are linked and harmonized. In order to run optimization and control systems in real-time, embedded systems communicate with each other wirelessly as part of a standardized architecture. This allows for increases in production output and optimized use of resources within the production process.

---

[5] Cf. Atzori, L. et. al. (2005). p. 2787.
[6] Cf. Härting, R. et. al. (2005). p. 10.
[7] Cf. VDI, VDE (2015). p. 12.
[8] Cf. VDI, VDE (2015). p. 12.
[9] Cf. VDI, VDE (2015). p. 12.

Lifecycle-Management, Continuous Engineering. [10]

Information flows that operate on an in-time basis between service, production, planning, engineering, design, development as well as direct customer feedback allow for efficient, target-oriented engineering and an optimized value chain.

Humans as part of the value chain [11]

As the case with earlier Industrial Revolutions, humans have not been replaced but instead have taken on a new role with new tasks as part of the value chain. Due to trends like automation and smart systems the role of humans is now to coordinate and orchestrate the interaction between different objects.

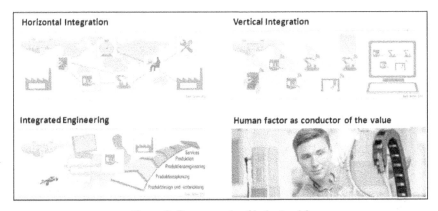

Figure 3: Four aspects of Industry 4.0

Source: VDI, VDE. (2015)

IoT as well as Industry 4.0 rest on two basis requirements. First, the increased connectivity of devices, machines and products. Second, on automation and the increasing intelligence of devices, machines and products. While IoT is focused on digitalization, Industry 4.0 concentrates on using digitalization to optimize the processes within a 'smart factory'. [12]

---

[10] Cf. VDI, VDE (2015). p. 12.
[11] Cf. VDI, VDE (2015). p. 12.
[12] Cf. Vogt, A. et. al. (2016). p. 2.

2.3 Technology Stack

'Smart, connected products require companies to build and support an entirely new technology infrastructure. This "technology stack" is made up of multiple layers, including new product hardware, embedded software, connectivity, a product cloud consisting of software running on remote servers, a suite of security tools, a gateway for external information sources, and integration with enterprise business systems.' [13]

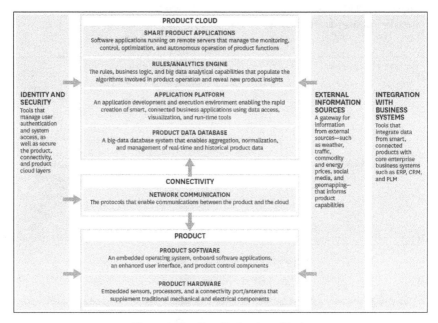

Figure 4: The New Technology Stack

Source: www.hbr.org (2014)

This new technology stack requires companies to align their processes, production and IT strategies with the requirements of Industry 4.0. The technology stack shown above in figure 4 illustrates the status of the product cloud as the backbone of this new smart industry. The following chapters will take an in-depth look at different cloud technologies and application possibilities.

---

[13] Cf. Porter, E. & Heppelmann, J. (2015). p. 101.

2.4 Cloud Computing

In order to allow for a better understanding of the strategic and economic evaluations later in this paper, the following sub-chapters will introduce the basics of Cloud Computing. The focus will be on basic principles relating to the flexibility and scalability of new IT technologies.

Definitions of Cloud Computing by experts vary to a great extent, however, all definitions share the view that Cloud Computing has to be divided into different levels and types. The following paragraphs will introduce the four main types and levels proposed in Cloud Computing theory.

Individual cloud types from different realms of science and business overlap to a high degree and one is well able to integrate them into an overall picture. Differences between the individual cloud types mostly relate to the location of the cloud solution which will be the focus of the following paragraphs.

2.4.1.1.1 Public Cloud

The most distinctive characteristic of the public cloud is the fact, that it does not operate in the IT-environment of a company. The majority of public cloud offers is provided by IT service operators or by manufacturers of IT equipment. A second distinctive characteristic, which differentiates the public cloud by the community cloud, is the availability of the offering. The public cloud in theory is open to any person or company. However, in reality entry barriers prevent precisely this. Where a company uses the public cloud, the company's infrastructure is not physically separated from the infrastructure of other customers. The division of infrastructure takes place on a purely logical level.[14]

The US-based NIST (National Institute of Standards and Technology) defines public cloud as follows: 'The cloud infrastructure is made available to the general public or a large industry group and is owned by an organization selling cloud.'[15]

2.4.1.1.2 Community Cloud

Where different companies or institutional customers have a similar or identical approach to Cloud Computing, but do not want to use the public cloud, a community cloud is a possible alternative. The community cloud is only accessible to those companies or institutions that have joined the respective group with its specific requirements. Common requirements among the customers may include aspects pertaining to data security and privacy. With regards to the operation of a community cloud solution there are two possibilities.

NIST defines the Community Cloud as 'the cloud infrastructure is shared by several organizations and supports a specific community that has shared concerns (e.g., mission,

---

[14] Cf. Armbrust, M. et al. (2010). p. 51.
[15] Cf. Mell, P. & Grance, T. (2011). p. 3.

6

security requirements, policy, and compliance considerations). It may be managed by the organizations or a third party and may exist on premise or off premise.' [16]

2.4.1.2 Private Cloud

The private cloud is only available for one individual company or institution. It's infrastructure requires a fully-automated virtual environment on which the cloud runs. The unique feature of the private cloud is the fact that the infrastructure is only available to the company that also operates it. In comparison to the previously-mentioned cloud types, there is not only a logical connection with the customer, instead the infrastructure is also physically located within the company network.[17]

The NIST definition for this variation reads as follows: 'The cloud infrastructure is provisioned for exclusive use by a single organization comprising multiple consumers (e.g., business units). It may be owned, managed, and operated by the organization, a third party, or some combination of them, and it may exist on or off premises.' [18]

2.4.1.3 Hybrid Cloud

In order to set up a hybrid cloud different types have to be combined with each other. For instance, one can combine public and private clouds in order to do so. In such a scenario the individual cloud types communicate via pre-determined interfaces which are offered by the provider of the public cloud. For the user this creates the impression of working within one single environment rather than working on two physically separated systems.

The NIST defines hybrid cloud as: 'The cloud infrastructure is a composition of two or more distinct cloud infrastructures (private, community, or public) that remain unique entities, but are bound together by standardized or proprietary technology that enables data and application portability (e.g., cloud bursting for load balancing between clouds)'. [19]

While in 2011 the private cloud was seen as a key industry trend (see Appendix, Figures 9) see Appendix, Figures 8), Gartner Group anticipates the combination of different cloud variations to play a key role within the next 2 to 5 years.

---

[16] Cf. Mell, P. & Grance, T. (2011). p. 7.
[17] Cf. Armbrust, M. et al. (2010). p. 51.
[18] Cf. Mell, P. & Grance, T. (2011). p. 7.
[19] Cf. Mell, P. & Grance, T. (2011). p. 7.

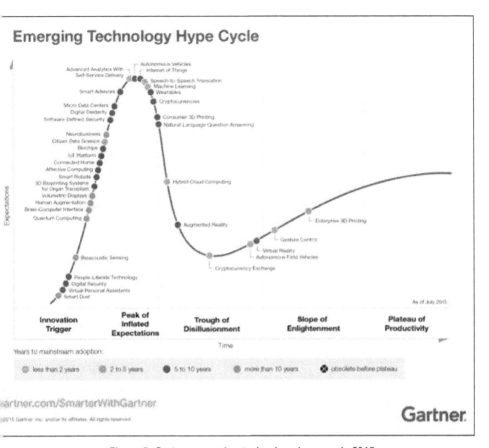

Figure 5: Gartner emerging technology hype cycle 2015

Source: www.blogs.gartner.com (2016)

The key question addressed by 'Gartner Emerging Technology Hype Cycle' is the anticipated development of key technological trends and how companies should accordingly deal with these technologies:

- 'Should you make an early move?'
- 'Is a moderate approach appropriate?'
- 'Should you wait for further maturation?' [20]

The strategic and commercial evaluation follows in chapters 3 and 4 of this paper.

---

[20] Cf. www.gartner.com (2016).

2.4.2 Cloud Levers

While the key difference among different cloud types is the location of the solution, different cloud levels can be divided according to the offered service. The following paragraphs will introduce the most important types: services infrastructure, platform and software.

2.4.2.1 Infrastructure as a Service (IaaS)[21]

The term Infrastructure as a Service refers to a Cloud Computing service that provides IT services as a basis for an IT infrastructure. Such services are commonly divided into three areas:

Storage: In order to save data, companies require storage space. In some instances storage can also be offered as its own separate cloud service: Data storage as a Service (DaaS).

Computing Resources: Computing resources are fully-automated, virtual environments for computing capacities that sometimes also rely on DaaS level storage capabilities in order to ensure a high degree of scalability.

Communications: Communications as a Service (CaaS) refers to the creation of a communication infrastructure.

2.4.2.2 Platform as a Service (PaaS)[22]

While the IaaS level is more geared towards administrators of IT systems, the PaaS level provides resources for the development of software and services. The conceptual design, programming, testing and packaging takes place 'on-premise', that means in the immediate environment of the developers. Upon completion of the development the software is not put into use on-premise, but instead on a PaaS platform chosen by the developers. Application programming interfaces (APIs) allow developers to use IaaS services and for the developed solutions to access the necessary storage resources and databases. This in turn ensures improved scalability.

2.4.2.3 Software as a service (SaaS)[23]

Apart from the levels that cater to administrators and developers, there is also a cloud solution for end users. This level is commonly called 'Software as a Service'. It provides the possibility for the end user to quickly and comfortably employ cloud services even without dedicated IT knowledge.

In this context the consumer has access to a variety of services including fairly simple ones like email services, extensive, standardized tools like CRM tools as well as special services

---

[21] Cf. Mell, P. & Grance, T. (2011). p. 7.
[22] Cf. Mell, P. & Grance, T. (2011). p. 7.
[23] Cf. BITKOM Arbeitskreis SaaS (2009). p. 3 ff.

designed on the PaaS level by developers. The main advantage for the customer is that he or she is no longer required to possess extensive IT knowledge. As the case with other levels of cloud services, availability details are determined through Service Level Agreements (SLAs).

2.4.3 Outsourcing of Cloud – Typical Pay System

After introducing the different types and levels of Cloud Computing, this chapter will introduce the payment systems of Cloud Computing. The payment system is an important feature of Cloud Computing as it mirrors the flexibility of the technology. In relation to Cloud Computing a commonly used term is 'pay as you go' which also exists in relation to mobile telecommunication contracts where customers only pay for the minutes and data volume they have effectively used. Contrary to 'pay as you go' in relation to mobile contracts, cloud customers do not pay in advance and also only pay for the services they effectively use. For companies that procure cloud services this payment system carries a number of advantages. IT departments within companies usually plan and predict which resources are needed for future periods. Figure 3 illustrates this process. It remains open, however, which time periods are covered by such forecasts. Following the forecasts the company has to plan how to procure and operate hardware, operating systems, licenses and other required IT resources.

3 Strategic Potentials of Cloud Systems

After the preceding chapters have shown the impact of Cloud Computing on Industry 4.0, the remainder of this termwork will address the strategic potential of cloud solutions.

Despite the impact on Industry 4.0 more than 50% of German companies have critical or neutral attitudes towards Cloud Computing (see figure 6).

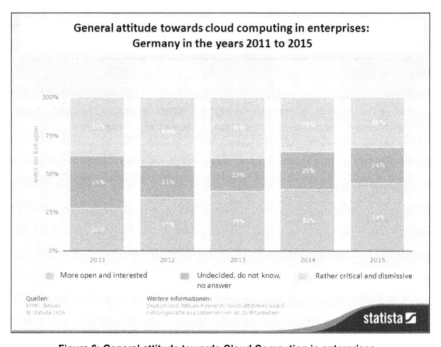

Figure 6: General attitude towards Cloud Computing in enterprises

Source: www.statista.de (B) (2016)

4 SWOT: Cloud and Industry 4.0

In evaluating the strategic impact of cloud strategies and the use of cloud services, one should not only take into account the potentials resulting from the technical capabilities described in chapter 2, but also the resulting potentials for Industry 4.0.

The following SWOT analysis evaluates strengths, weaknesses, opportunities and threats of the entire cloud environment:

- Cloud Outsourcing/ Usage of Cloud Suppliers
- As a Service functionalities
- Indirect potentials of Industry 4.0

4.1 Strengths

Flexibility: flexible and scalable according to changing needs and requirements.

Cost savings: billing systems based on actual use: Pay as you use.

No licensing & hardware invest: included in flat charge.[24]

Internet: broadband internet at adequate cost and with premium availability.[25]

Support and Administration: included in flat charge.[26]

Availability: Supplier Cloud Service are always on.

Mobility: Data stored in the cloud can be accessed from virtually anywhere with an internet connection.

Speed: Shorter implementation times and evergreening models.

4.2 Weaknesses

Legacy of established systems

Small and medium-sized organizations can step in faster to use the benefits of the cloud than larger companies which may have complicated legacy systems.

Technology Maturity

45% of CIOs perceive IoT technologies as not mature.[27]

User attitude and control: For many, the idea of giving up control of the hardware that carries business critical data and outsourcing confidential customer data to a third party is an unsettling concept.

---

[24] Cf. BITKOM Arbeitskreis SaaS (2009). p. 9.
[25] Cf. BITKOM Arbeitskreis SaaS (2009). p. 4.
[26] Cf. BITKOM Arbeitskreis SaaS (2009). p. 9.
[27] Cf. Capgemini (2016). p. 14.

4.3 Opportunities

In house IT personal: Additional capacities by using IT employees, that have an affinity for the products and processes of the company, to realize the potentials of IoT and Industry 4.0 (smart factory).[28] Special know-how is not required as the focus lies on key competences.

Agility and flexibility: Smaller firms are nimble and thus more easily able to move to the cloud and take advantage of Cloud Computing's many cost-saving benefits.

Growth in cloud services: Cloud services will continue to grow with increasing competition from both established players and new entrants. Some observers estimate that the cloud market in Germany will top EUR 20 billion in 2016 (EUR 15 billion in 2016).[29]

Data Protection & Security: Legal requirements and expectations within society will lead to attainment of high-level standards based on offering of professional Cloud Services providers.

4.4 Threats

In house IT Personnel: Many IT professionals will need to re-invent themselves as organizations do away with expensive IT departments.

Skills shortage: Lack of skilled professionals for IoT is one of the main obstacles for digitalization.[30]

Data Protection & Security: Requirements with regards to patent protection, data privacy and data security make high demands on the choice of cloud services provider and the appropriate cloud solution.

4.5 Service Capacity of Industry 4.0[31]

In 1994 KMU Aalen carried out an online-survey among 133 German-speaking experts for Industry 4.0. Table 1 summarizes key findings of the survey:

Table 1: Service Capacity of Industry 4.0 – KMU Online Survey

78,9 %	estimate the general service capacity of Industry 4.0 for companies to be relatively high.
67,0 %	estimate the potential for optimization of time of production to be relatively high.
66,2 %	estimate the potential for the optimization of setup-time to be relatively high.
69,1 %	estimate the potential for the optimization of idle time to be relatively high.
63,9 %	estimate the potential for the optimization of time-to-market time to be relatively high.
75,0 %	regard the individual and specific requirements of their customers as relatively high.
80,4 %	believe that Industry 4.0 will strengthen the production of individualized goods.
70,2 %	are convinced that Industry 4.0 will most likely have a relatively high impact on the degree of automation within the production process.

---

[28] Cf. BITKOM Arbeitskreis SaaS (2009). p. 13.
[29] Cf. Statistica (A) (2016).
[30] Cf. Capgemini (2016). p. 14.
[31] Cf. Härting, R. et. al. (2005). p. 19 f.

5 Economic Aspects of Classic IT

Buzzwords of Indstrie 4.0, IoT and Cloud Computing such as dynamics, flexibility, real time, virtual world, 'X as a Service' indicate that the IT sector will experience significant increases in efficiency. This trend, however, contradicts the current, fairly static pricing models used in IT projects such as Return of Investment (RoI) and Total Cost of Ownership (TCO).

5.1 Profitability Analysis - Classic Methods

In the early stages IT projects initially create costs, before these costs are set off at a later stage through the benefit generated by the project and a profit is generated. The benefit for the customer can come in varied forms and shapes such as cost savings or increases in productivity for the customer. It is also possible for the project to have a positive impact on the client's revenues. In general IT projects are regarded as successful when benefits exceed efforts.[32]

To determine whether this is the case, there are a number of different methods such as static, dynamic and value-based approaches (see figure 7).

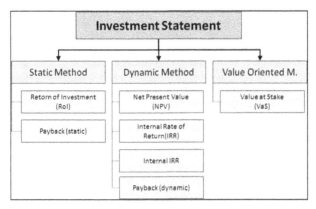

Figure 7: Investment calculation method in IT

Source: Inspired by Brugger (2009) p. 141.

The most often used methods are Return of Investment (RoI) und Net Present Value (NPV).

5.1.1 Basic - Static method - RoI

For individual IT projects the calculation of RoI by setting benefit and costs into relation of one another has proven to be successful.[33] The term benefit in this context refers to cost

---

[32] Cf. Brugger (2009). p. 139.
[33] Cf. Brugger (2009). p. 141 ff.

14

savings or revenues or a combination of both. Costs refer to Capex and operating costs for the system, software and the infrastructure. Below the formula to calculate RoI:

$$ROI(IT\ invest) = \frac{cost\ cutting + earnings}{investment\ costs + operating\ costs} = \frac{value}{cost} \quad (1)$$

5.1.2 Basic - Dynamic method - NPV

This method is the by far most commonly-used method to evaluate an investment. It takes into account all payments that arise in connection with a specific investment. The net present value is the result of all in- and outflows which are discounted in order to reflect the time value of money. In addition, the investment sum and potential capital gains at the end of the project are taken into account.[34]

$$C(IT\ invest) = -I_0 + \sum_{t=1}^{n}(R_t) * (1 + i)^{-t} + L * (1 + i)^{-T} \quad (2)$$

C: NPV
I: Invest
T: Viewing period
R_t: Reflux in period t
L: Liquidation proceeds
i: Interest rate

Due to their static nature ROI as well as NPV are not suited to take into account the typical dynamic nature of IT projects. Besides, it is difficult to integrate full costs into these models. The shortcomings of the static methods have led to the development of methods that are specifically suited to IT projects such as the TCO model introduced in the following chapter.

5.2 IT cost-based profitability analysis on TCO[35]

Profitability analysis for IT projects has become an important decision-making tool for the IT departments of companies. The key concept is to capture all costs that charge the project-specific budget. On the one hand, this includes overall IT costs, on the other hand costs for individual projects, products or service offerings. In order to determine the overall costs, Gartner Group developed the so-called Total Costs of Ownership model in the mid 1980s. Through the use of this model, all costs within the lifetime-cycle of an IT investment can be recorded with the ultimate aim to evaluate the economic feasibility of the investment. In order to do this all costs pertaining to the investment are collected and then valued.

Thanks to the overarching view of all costs, not only direct costs which are documented on the basis of bills and receipts, but also indirect costs, i.e. such costs which are not directly allocable to a specific department, are taken into account. Traditional concepts (e.g. internal

---

[34] Cf. Brugger (2009). p. 195 ff.
[35] Cf. Wild, M. & Herges, S. (2000). p. 3 ff.

cost allocation) do not take into account indirect costs. Therefore, one can conclude that traditional concepts have a lower degree of transparency and conceal the actual costs of IT infrastructure. The aim of the TCO method is to remedy this problem of lack of transparency. Thanks to the overall view of costs, companies can compare their costs with industry-wide benchmarks and competitors. This allows companies to ascertain their competitive position with regards to IT infrastructure costs. Nowadays, decisions concerning IT infrastructure in most companies are taken by top management. The TCO method allows top management executives to take well-informed strategic decisions. While relevant, this term paper will not specifically address 'TCO Model v4.0 (see Appendix Figure 9- Distributed Computing Chart of Accounts'[36] (Gartner Group), as it would exceed the scope.

Commonly-used TCO models include models by Gartner, Forrester and Meta Group. These models overlap in some regards, however, it is difficult to compare them directly. Further, the models do only take into account costs but not benefits.

6 Conclusion of adaption fields of action

The previous chapter has presented different approaches to the evaluation of IT investments and their potential success. As Cloud Computing services differ significantly from traditional IT services, these previously-mentioned methods have to be adjusted. Such adjustments, however, have to be carried out in a way that still allows for cloud services to be compared with on-premise solutions. The following sub-chapters will list the relevant drivers that should be integrated in RoI and NPV models and have an impact on indirect costs that are part of the TCO model. The drivers will reference in particular chapters 4.1 Strengths and 4.2 Opportunities.

6.1 Speed

Through the adaption of Cloud Computing it is possible to decrease the costs for the introduction of new services. This relates to the fact, that the time between the decision and the actual implementation is reduced through the selection of pre-defined services. Further, there are cost effects by transferring Capex costs to Opex costs. Further cost reductions can be realized as development environments can now more quickly be turned into productive environments.

6.2 Capex vs. Opex

Capex costs can be reduced as some Capex costs are replaced by Opex costs. This translates into a faster RoI and an improved NPV.

---

[36] Cf. Wild, M. & Herges, S. (2000). p. 15 ff.

6.3 Optimization of Total Costs

An optimization of total costs of cloud services is possible as the end-user is able to precisely define which services he requires. An example is the integration of the Office365 suite within a company where the IT department is able to carry out the administration of the service and therefore to respond to the needs of the company.[37]

6.4 Scalability and flexibility

As the systems offered are already pre-configured by the providers, the customer can concentrate on planning and if needed rely on the pre-configured systems. There is no longer the need to order hard- and software. Where a company decides to procure a service from the SaaS-level, time savings are significant as the service can be provided within a very short time. This service can then be customized according to specific needs and is ready to use. Before the introduction of cloud services, companies would have to take into account a longer planning phase as well as more time for the order and installation process. Therefore, the implementation on-premise would take much longer than the procurement of a cloud service. In addition, in case of the immediate need for additional resources customers can directly procure such and in this way are able to avoid the loss of revenues.

Flexibility in general is one of the most important aspects of Cloud Computing. Companies can not only chose among different cloud services but providers can also customize individual aspects of products in order to suit their needs. The monetary benefit of customizing products according to customers' needs can also be measured.

6.5 Profit maximization

Through the use of cost-efficient services, profits can be increased. While this is not an entirely new revelation, Cloud Computing can also decrease the initial invest. This is of particular relevance to software developers who are able by using PaaS to minimize their invest during the development stage. Where the product is successful, however, the use of resources can be increased. Due to the flexibility at the onset of the development stage, higher profit margins can be realized when the product is sold.

6.6 Meeting regulations and guidelines

For companies it becomes possible to pass on the responsibility for CO_2 emissions that result from the operation of computing centers to the providers of cloud services. The providers again, have to ensure that their computing centers operate cost-efficiently and

---

[37] Cf. BITKOM Arbeitskreis SaaS (2009). p. 37.

environment-friendly. Thanks to the concentration on the providers' computing centers it is possible to employ cost- and energy-efficient technologies that lower the price of the services. Furthermore, cloud service providers are seeking to follow laws and regulations concerning data privacy and security in order to protect their services from third party attacks.

Lastly, thanks to the use of green IT services costs for electricity, cooling and emissions can be reduced which is a direct monetary benefit for any company.

6.7 Adaptation of the direct and indirect costs of TCO

6.7.1 Adaptation of the direct costs of TCO

Through the use of Cloud Computing direct costs can be significantly reduced as the customer no longer has to pay for costs arising from hard- and software. The company procures a service from a cloud service provider who is now responsible for this cost type. However, this cost category is replaced by a new category. While companies no longer have to keep track of hard- and software costs, they now have to take into account the costs for the use of cloud services. That means that the cost type changes and become now 100% service-type costs. Further, there is the need for adjustments within operational departments as companies less fewer employees that maintain the on-premise infrastructure. Accordingly, salary costs for such employees decrease. However, there now also exist new divisions that deal with the administration of cloud services. Such new divisions replace former fields such as support and database management functions. Administrative costs do not require a lot of adjustments. Nevertheless, due to the different nature of the cloud service the structure within this cost category also changes. Initially, one can assume that all IT employees will require additional training while the costs for administration and finance will decrease.

6.7.2 Adaptation of the indirect costs of TCO

The second part of the TCO model deals with the indirect costs of the entire IT infrastructure or an individual project. The costs for end-user activity remains unaffected due to the use of Cloud Computing. With regards to downtimes, the specific nature of the cloud has to be born in mind. Most cloud service providers do not schedule downtimes for their services. Whereas downtimes for on-premise infrastructure creates costs for the customer due to a possible production stop, downtimes for cloud-services often allow the customer to claim damages. Compensation for downtimes will be covered by the SLAs of the provider and can include a variety of compensation models from the refund of monthly costs to penalty payments.

6.7.3 Cloud-related adjustments of the TCO model

From the matters discussed in Sections 6.1 to 6.7.2, the result is indicated in Figure 8 as adjustments for the calculation of TCO for cloud solutions in outsourcing. The basic structure of the TCO model by Gartner is shown in appendix figure 11.

18

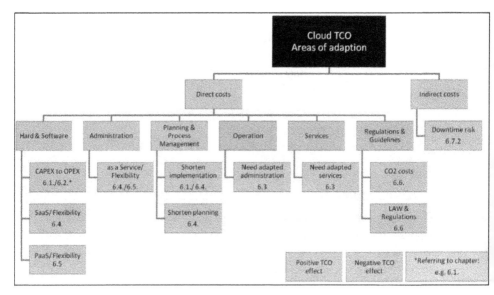

Figure 8: Cloud-related changes of the TCO model

Source: Own representation

19

7 Conclusion

As illustrated by the preceding chapters, Cloud Computing is the backbone and enabler as part of the architecture stack of the Internet of Things and Industry 4.0. This requires the German manufacturing industry to embrace cloud technology in order to ensure its ability to compete globally in the future. Especially global customers have a high demand for the benefits of Industry 4.0, in the B2B realm, as well as in the B2C field where increased flexibility, virtualization, personalization of products and shorter innovation circles are some of the key trends.

Particularly against the backdrop of decreasing or stagnating IT budgets within the last few years, cloud-based solutions present clear opportunities.[38] In order to take advantage of these opportunities it is mandatory that companies investigate how to use the strategic potentials of implementations in Industry 4.0 as well as remain open for the potentials of hybrid cloud solutions.

Through the adaption of the classic valuation methods such as ROI and NPV to suit cloud services and the adjustment of direct and indirect cost drivers within the TCO method, a new economic valuation tool for cloud services is created, that allows for comparisons with on-premise solutions.

The integration of the benefit for Industry 4.0 as part of the valuation method for cloud solutions has exceeded the scope of this paper and needs to be addressed separately. Further, additional aspects of cloud and 'as a Service' solutions remain to be discussed.

In my daily job I am often asked how German companies can obtain the necessary resources and competencies in order to embrace Industry 4.0. Through the use of cloud solutions, IT professionals that are already familiar with the companies products and processes will become available. Those are exactly those professionals that have the ideal basis to help companies realize the potentials of IoT and Industry 4.0 (smart company).

---

[38] Cf. Capgemini (2016). p. 9.

List of Literature and Sources

Atzori, L. et. al. (2010). *The Internet of Things: A survey*. In: Computer Networks, Nr. 54 / 2010

Armbrust, M. et al. (2010). *A View of Cloud Computing*. Within: Communications of the ACM, Vol 53. Nr. 4 / 2010

BITKOM Arbeitskreis SaaS (2009*). Leitfaden für Saas-Anwender*. Berlin: BITKOM

Brugger, R. (2009). *Der IT Business Case*. Berlin: Springer Verlag

Capgemini (2016). *Studie IT-Trends 2016*. Berlin: Capgemini Deutschland Holding GmbH

Dorst, W. (2012): Fabrik *und Produktionsprozesse der Industry 4.0*. Within: IM Die Fachzeitschrift für Information, Management & Consulting, Nr. 3/2010.

Härting, R. et. al. (2005). *Nutzenpotentiale von Industry 4.0*. Nordstedt: BoD

Mell, P. / Grance, T. (2011). *The NIST Definition of Cloud Computing*. USA: National Institute of Standards and Technology

Porter, E. / Heppelmann, J. (2015). *How smart, connected products are transforming companies*. In: Harvard Business Review, October 2016

VDI, VDE (2015). *Referenzarchitekturmodell Industry 4.0 (RAMI 4.0)*. Düsseldorf: Verein Deutscher Ingenieure e.V. VDI/ VDE Gesellschaft

Vogt, A. et. al. (2016). *Industry 4.0 / Internet of Things Vendor Benchmark 2016*. Deutsche Telekom: White Paper

Wild, M. / Herges, S. (2000). *Total Cost of Ownership (TCO) – Ein Überblick*. Mainz: Universität Mainz

Internet Sources

https://bestemnetwork.com/2016/03/29/innovation-and-productivity-with-4th-industrial-revolution/ - Tiel: Innovation and productivity with 4th Industrial Revolution - Request date: 2016/07/13

http://blogs.gartner.com/smarterwithgartner/files/2015/10/EmergingTech_Graphic.png - Titel: Gartner emerging technology hype cycle 2015 - Request date: 2016/07/12

http://www.computerwoche.de/a/gartner-hype-cycle-die-mutter-aller-prognosen,2492728 – Titel: Gartner emerging technology hype cycle 2001 - Request date: 2016/07/14

http://www.gartner.com/technology/research/methodologies/hype-cycle.jsp - Title: Gartner emerging technology hype cycle 2015 - Request date: 2016/07/13

https://hbr.org/2015/10/how-smart-connected-products-are-transforming-companies - Title: HBR – How smart connected products are transforming companies (October 2015) – Request date: 2016/07/13 http://de.statista.com/statistik/daten/studie/252728/umfrage/geschaetztes-historisches-bruttoinlandsprodukt-der-welt-nach-regionen/ - (A) – Titel: Geschaetztes-historisches-bruttoinlandsprodukt-der-welt-nach-regionen - Request date: 2016/07/12

statistic_id175463_generelle-einstellung-zum-thema-cloud-computing-in-deutschland-bis-2015.pn http://de.statista.com/statistik/daten/studie/175463/umfrage/grundeinstellung-gegenueber-cloud-computing-in-deutschland/ - (B) – Titel: Grundeinstellung gegenueber Cloud Computing in Deutschland - Request date: 2016/07/14

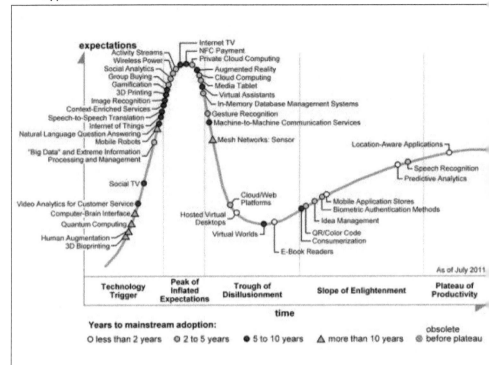

Figure 9: Gartner emerging technology hype cycle 2011

Source: www.computerwoche.de (2016)

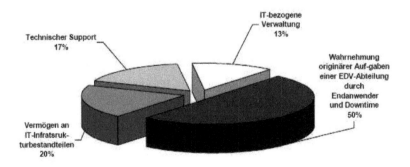

Figure 10: Basic classification of TCO on their base cost factors

Source: Wild, M. / Herges, S. (2000). p. 5.

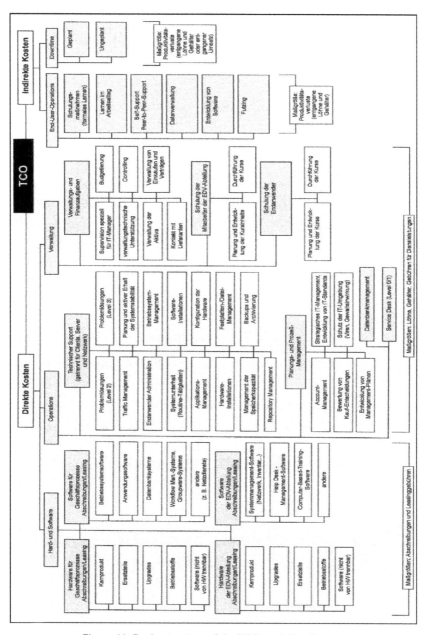

Figure 11: Basic structure of the TCO model by Gartner

Source: Wild, M. / Herges, S. (2000) p. 8.

www.ingramcontent.com/pod-product-compliance
Lightning Source LLC
La Vergne TN
LVHW042309060326
832902LV00009B/1365